# *world of beauty*

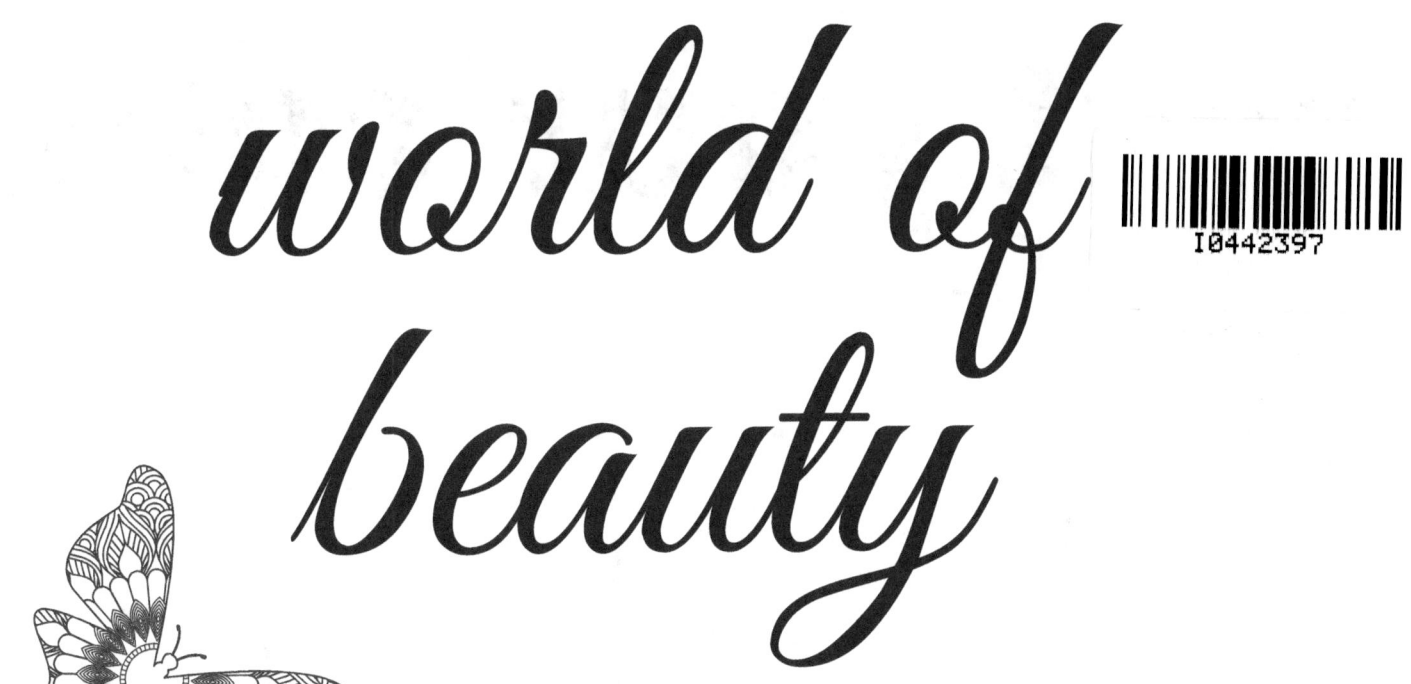

## this coloring book belongs too

. . . . . . . . . . .

# test your color

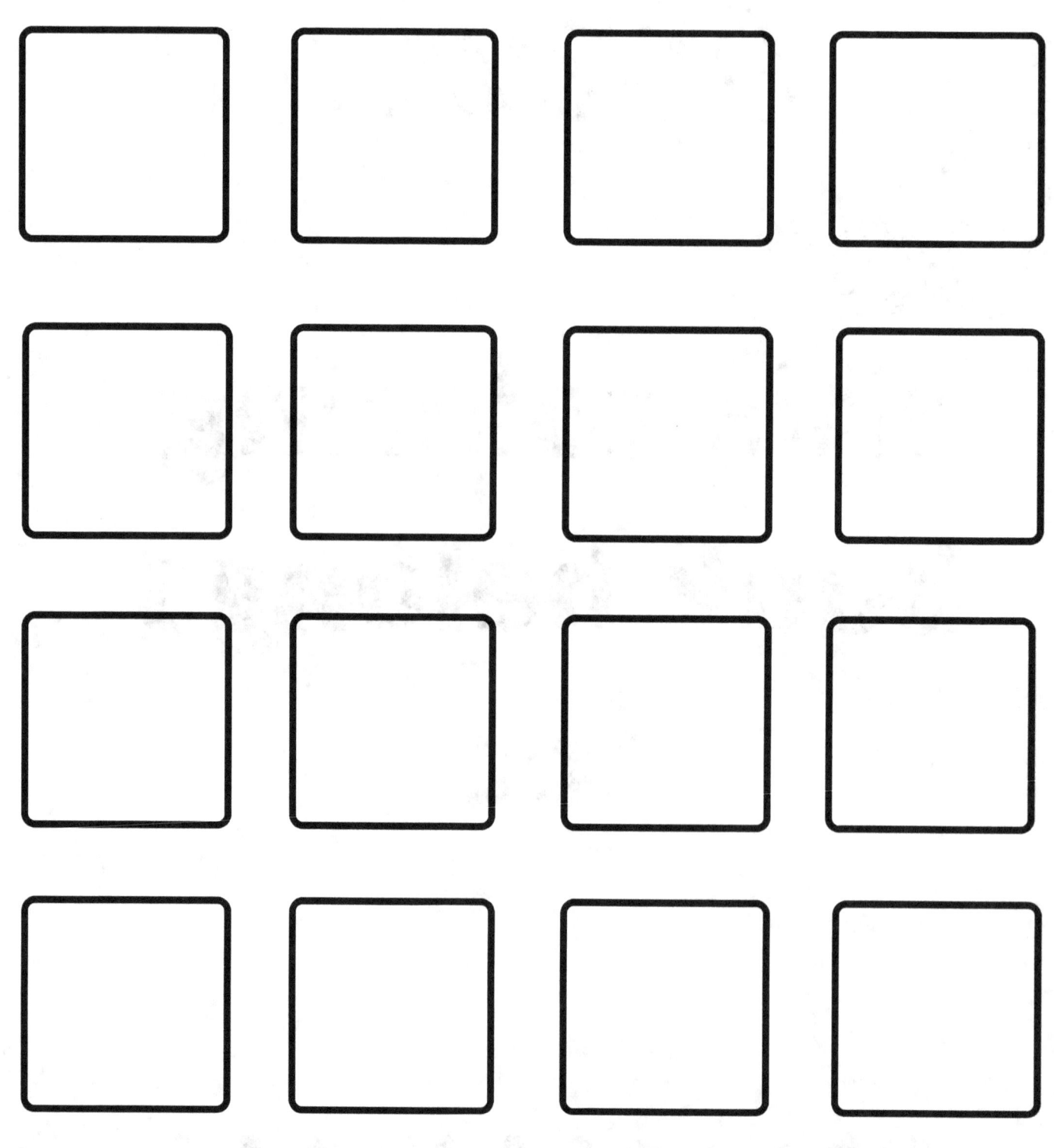

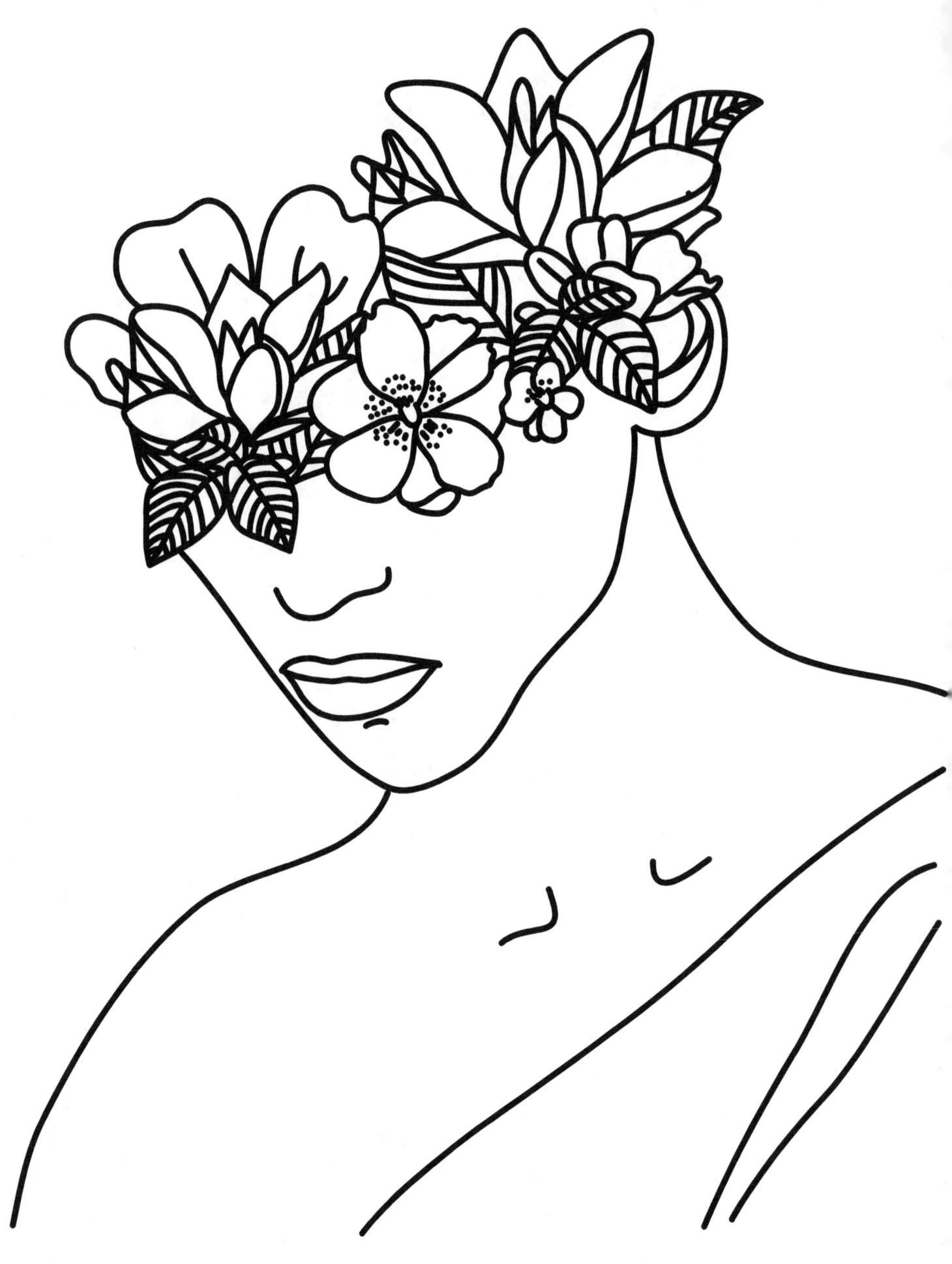

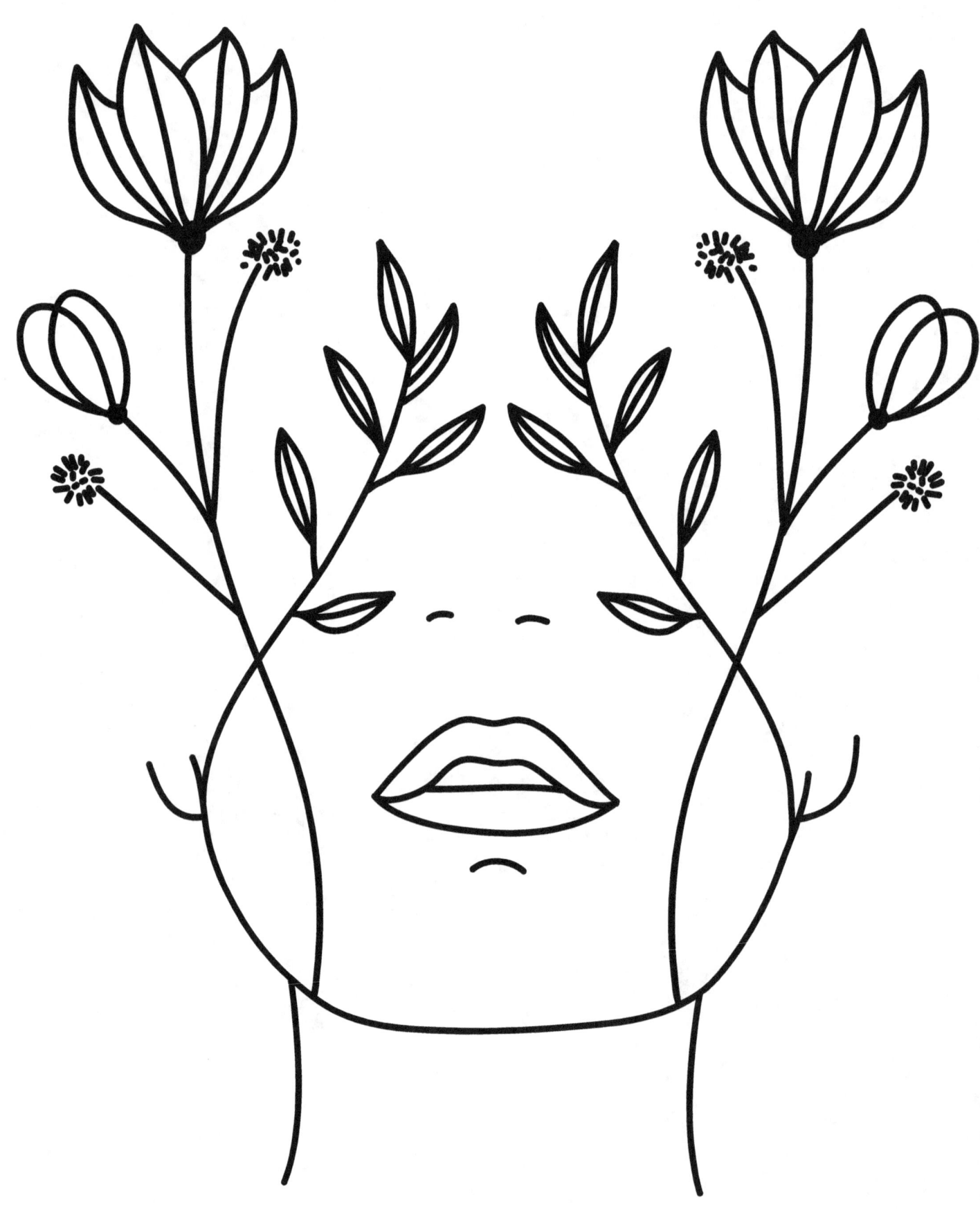

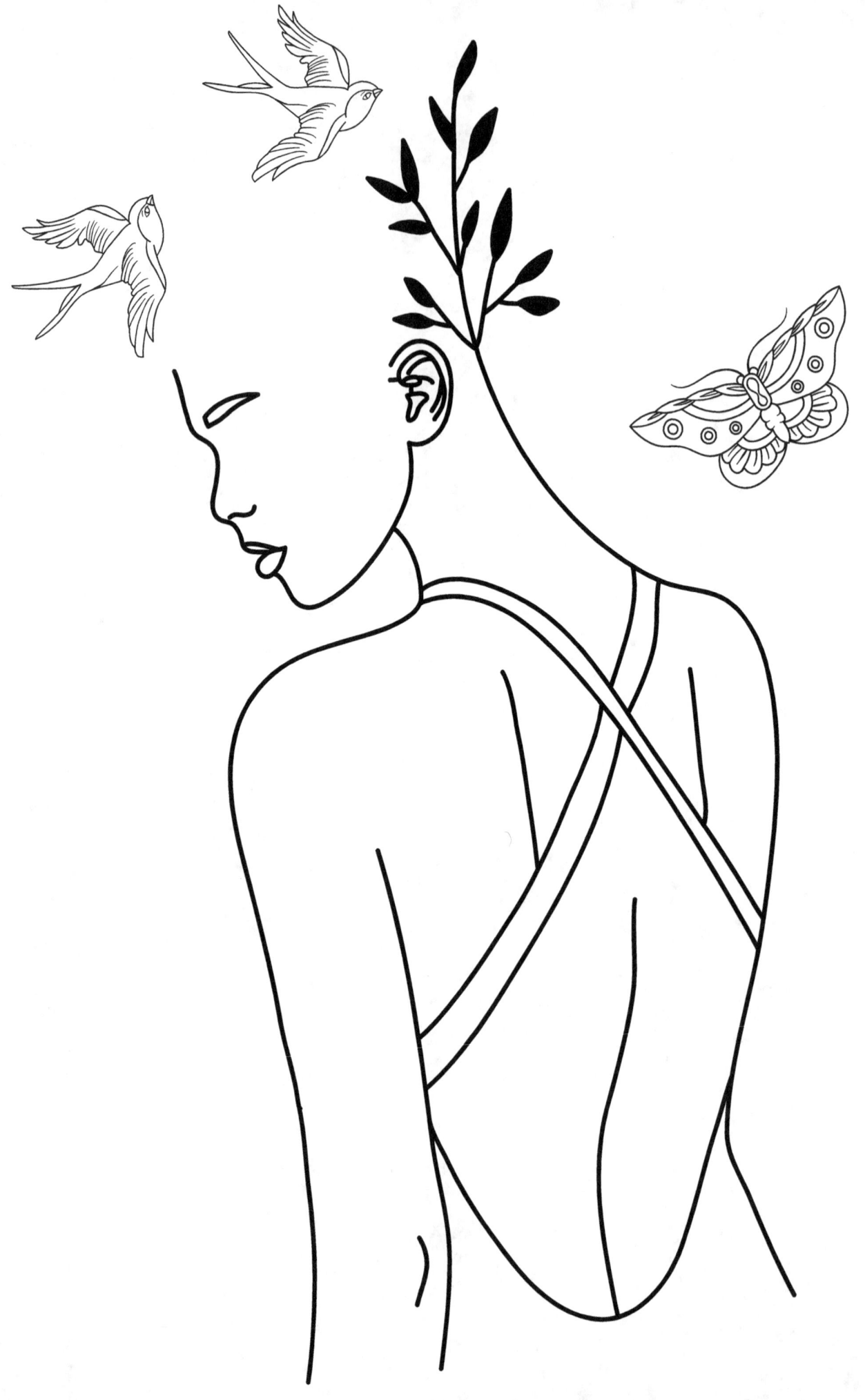

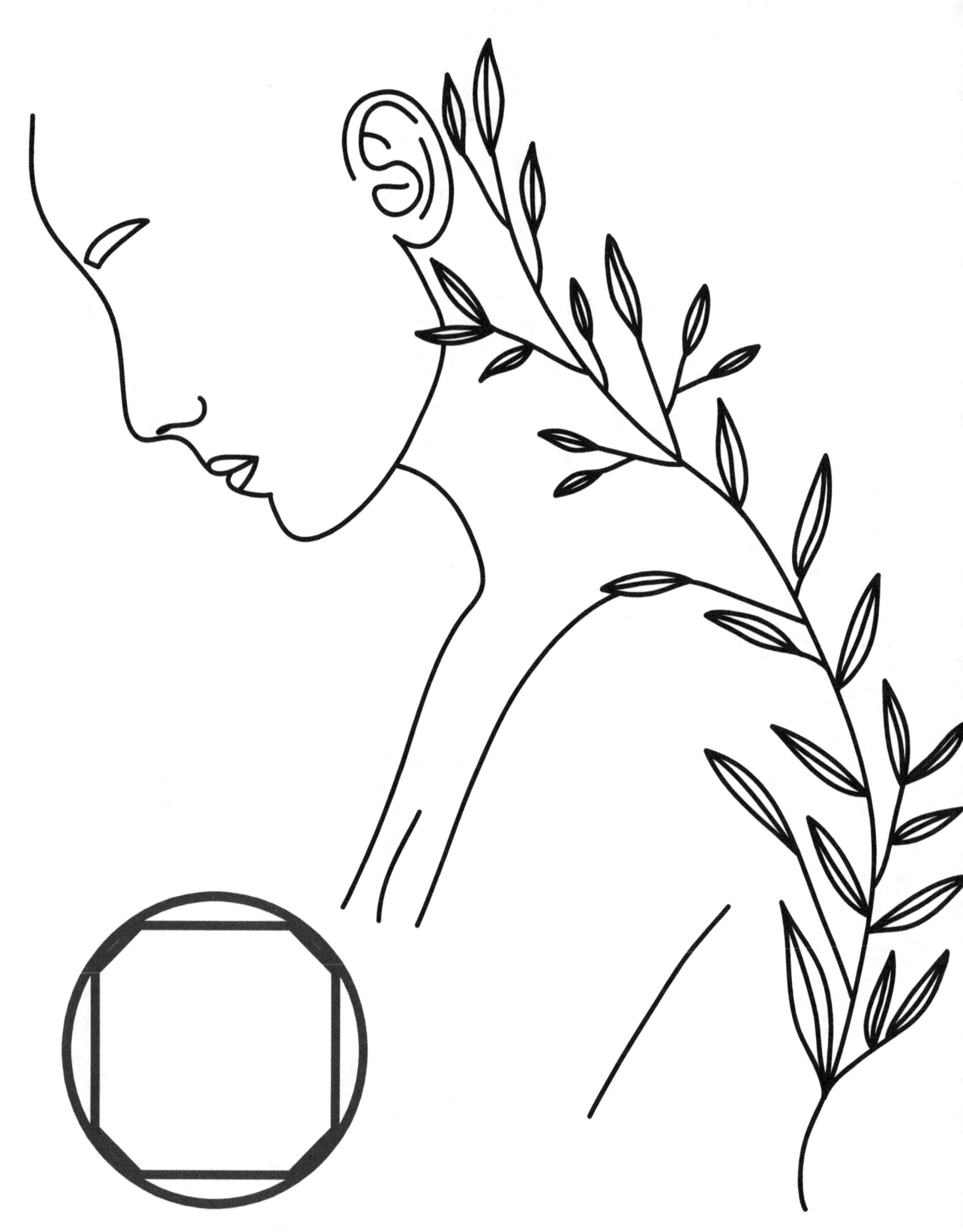

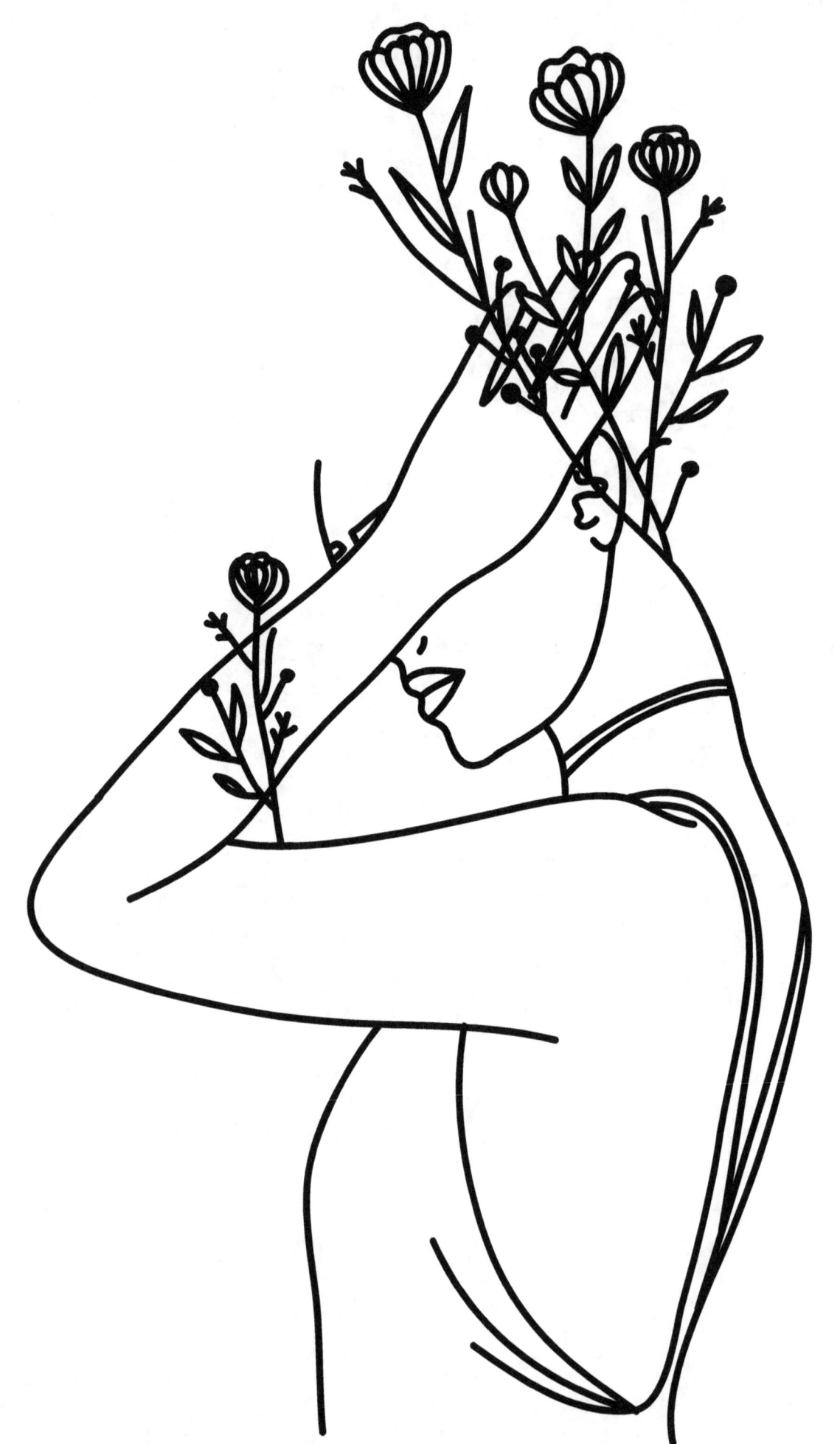

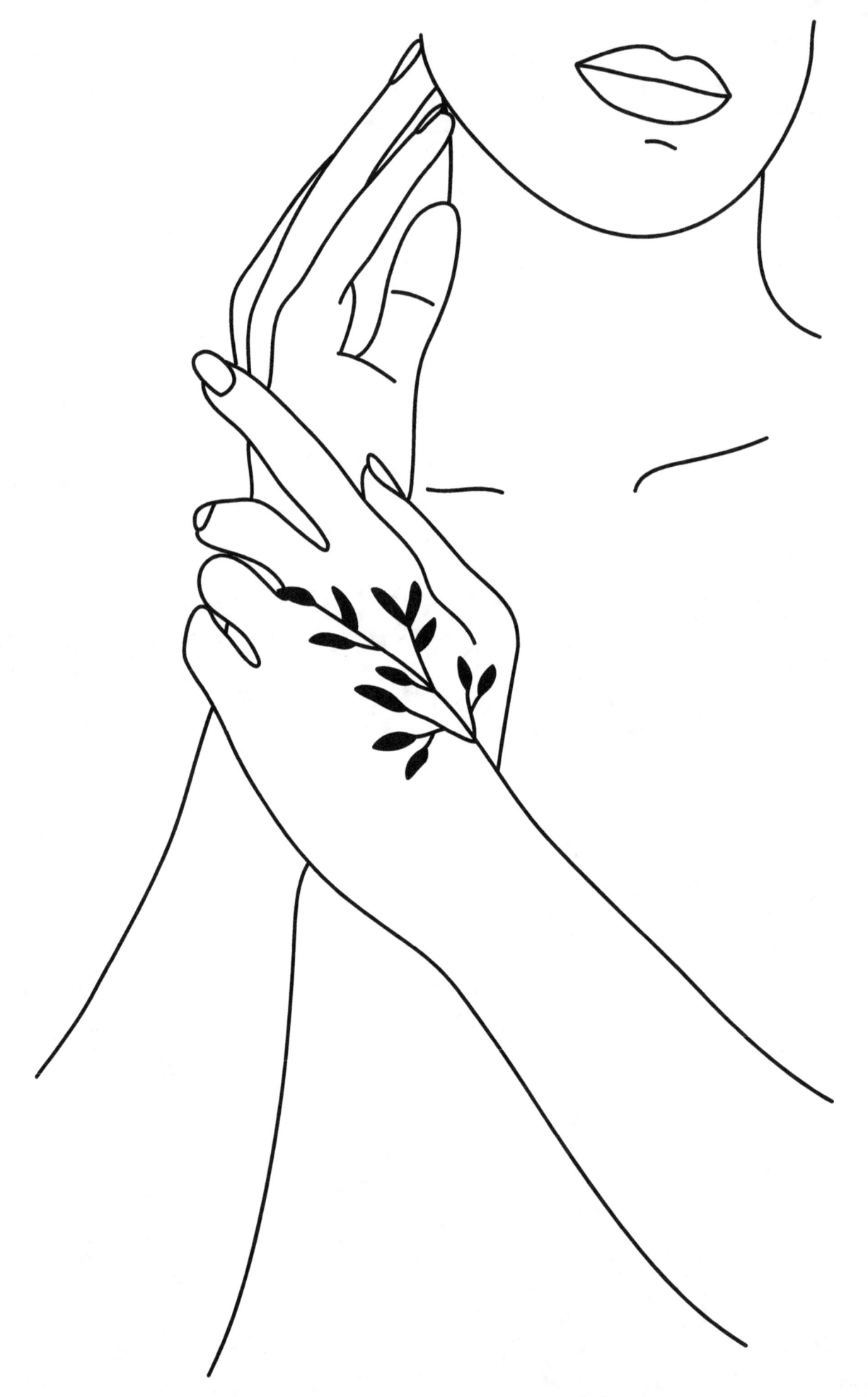

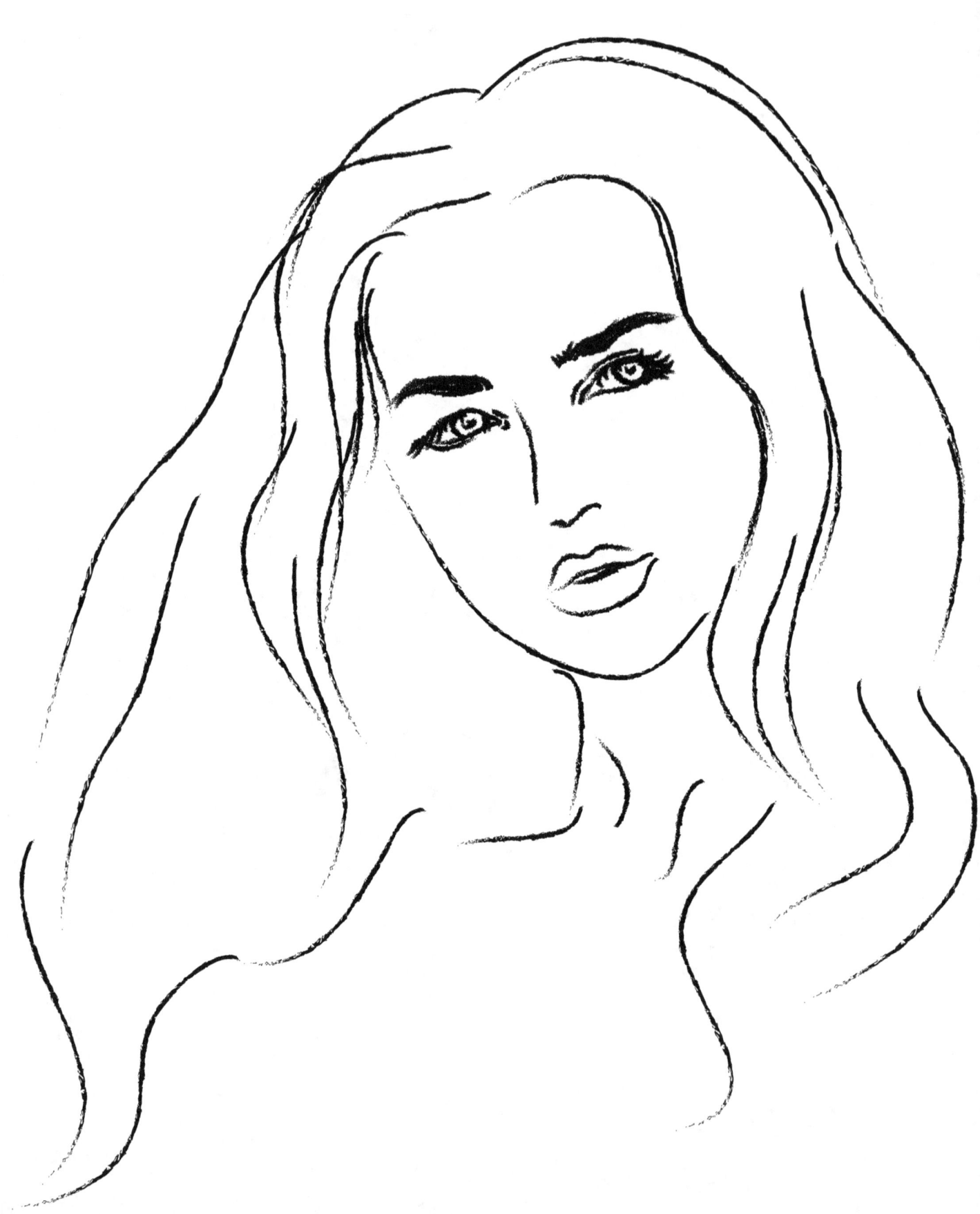

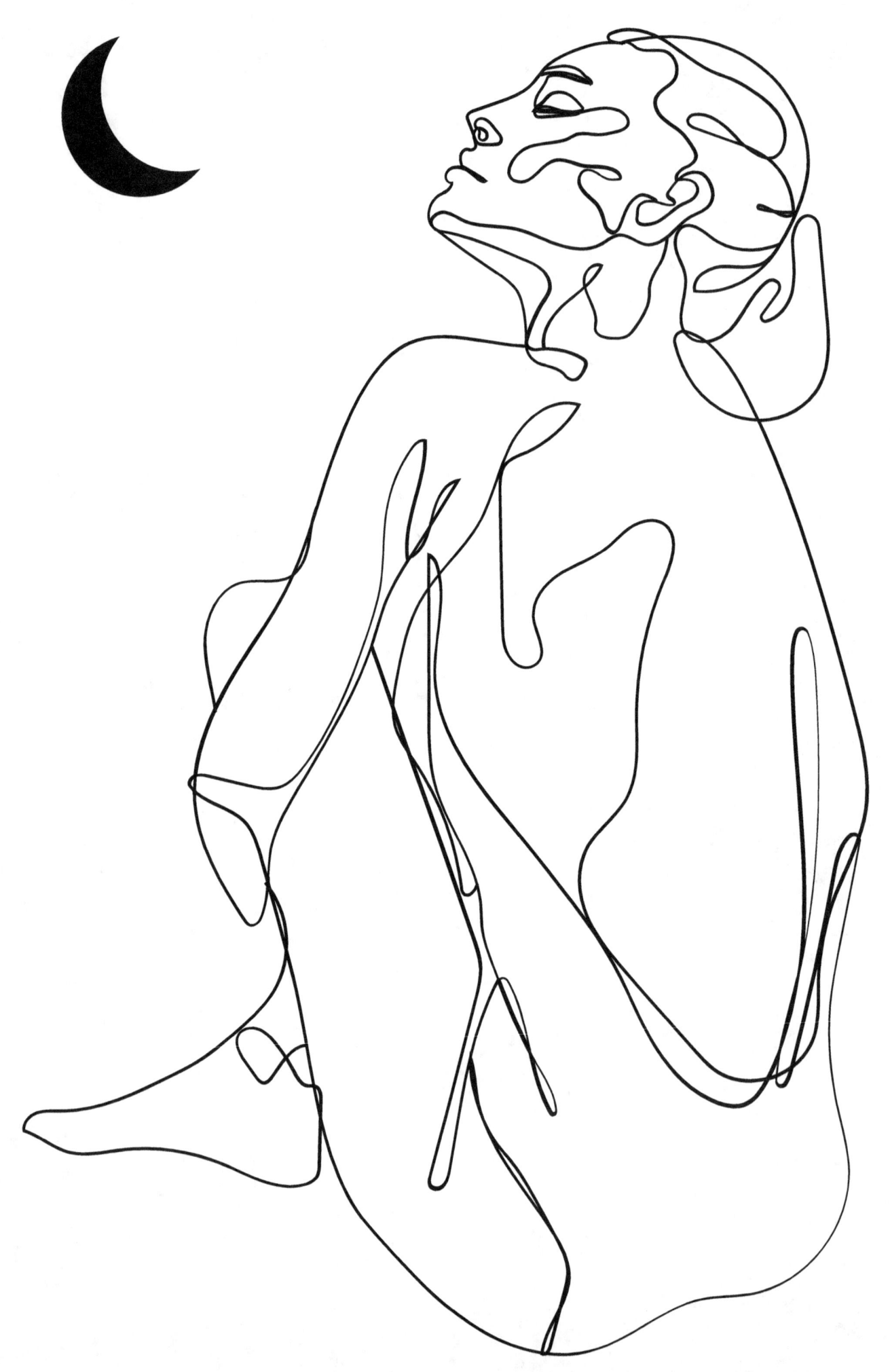

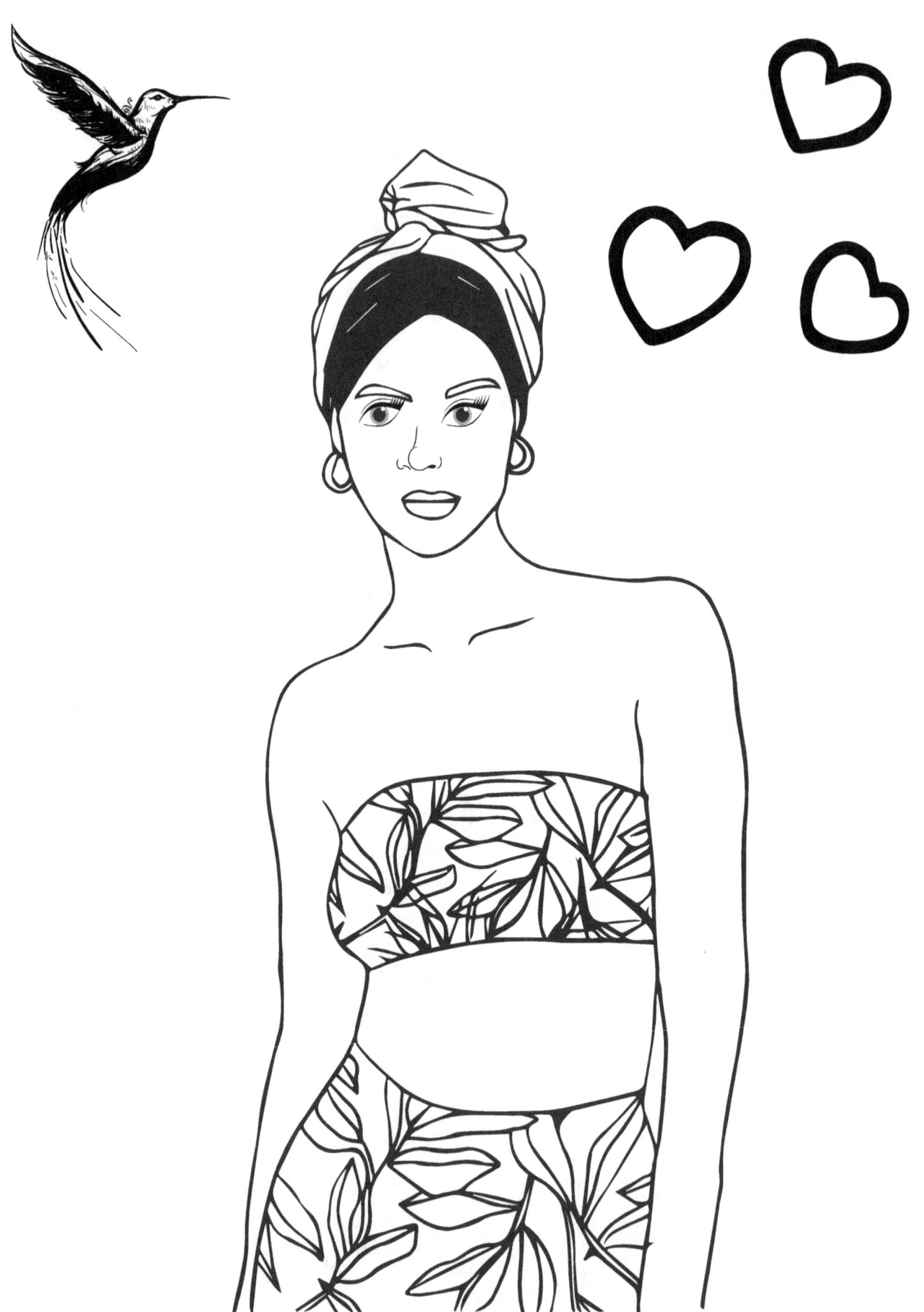

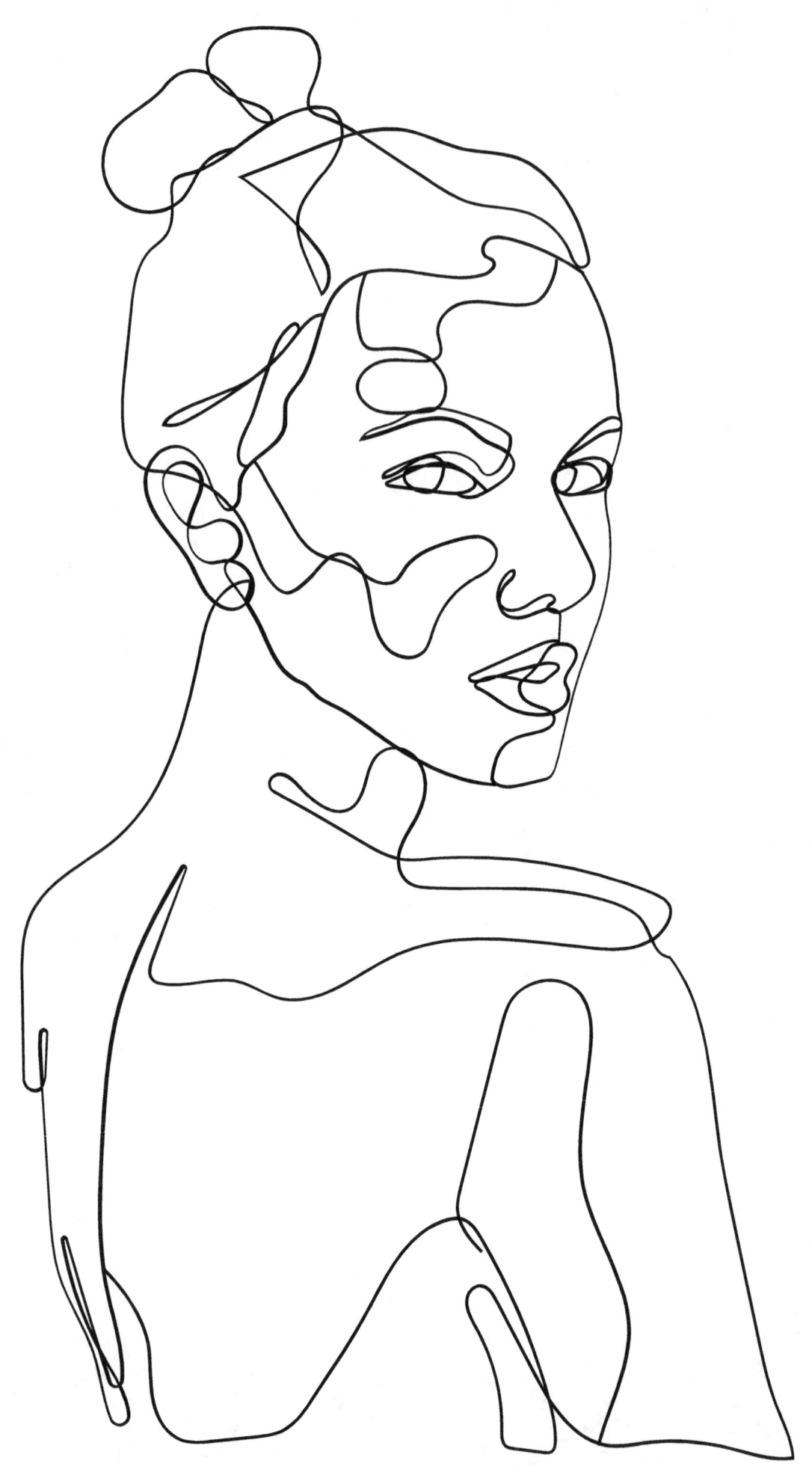

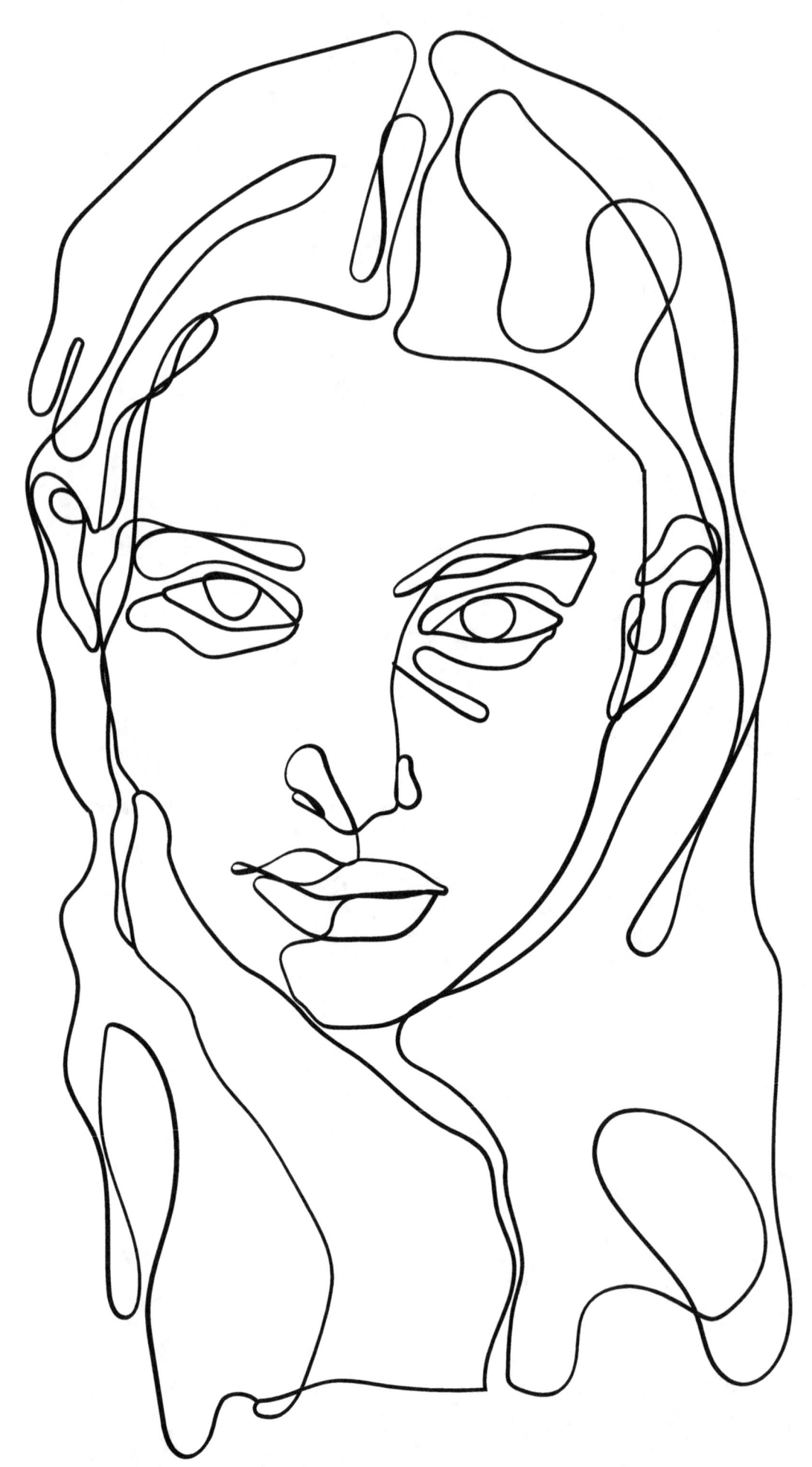

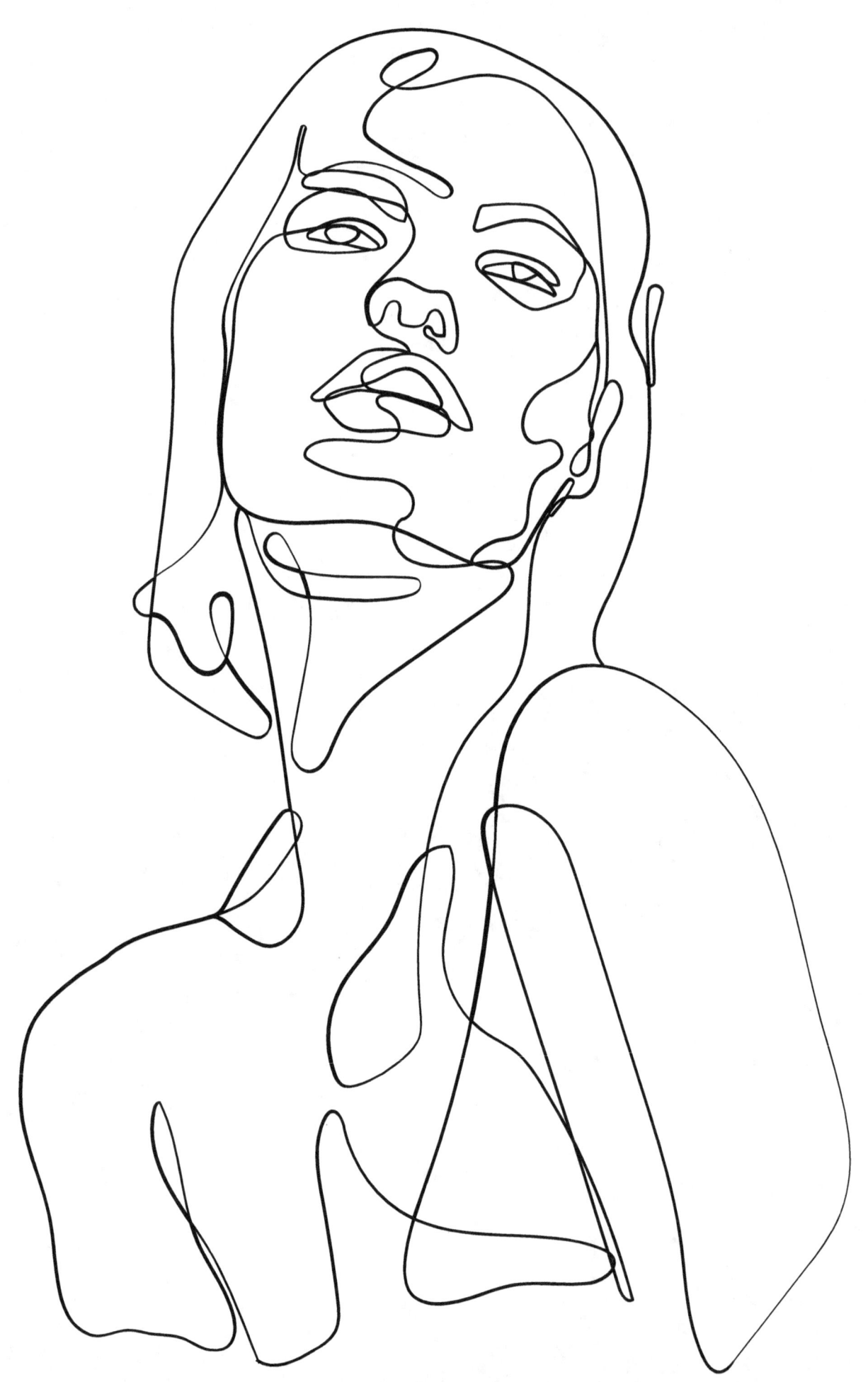

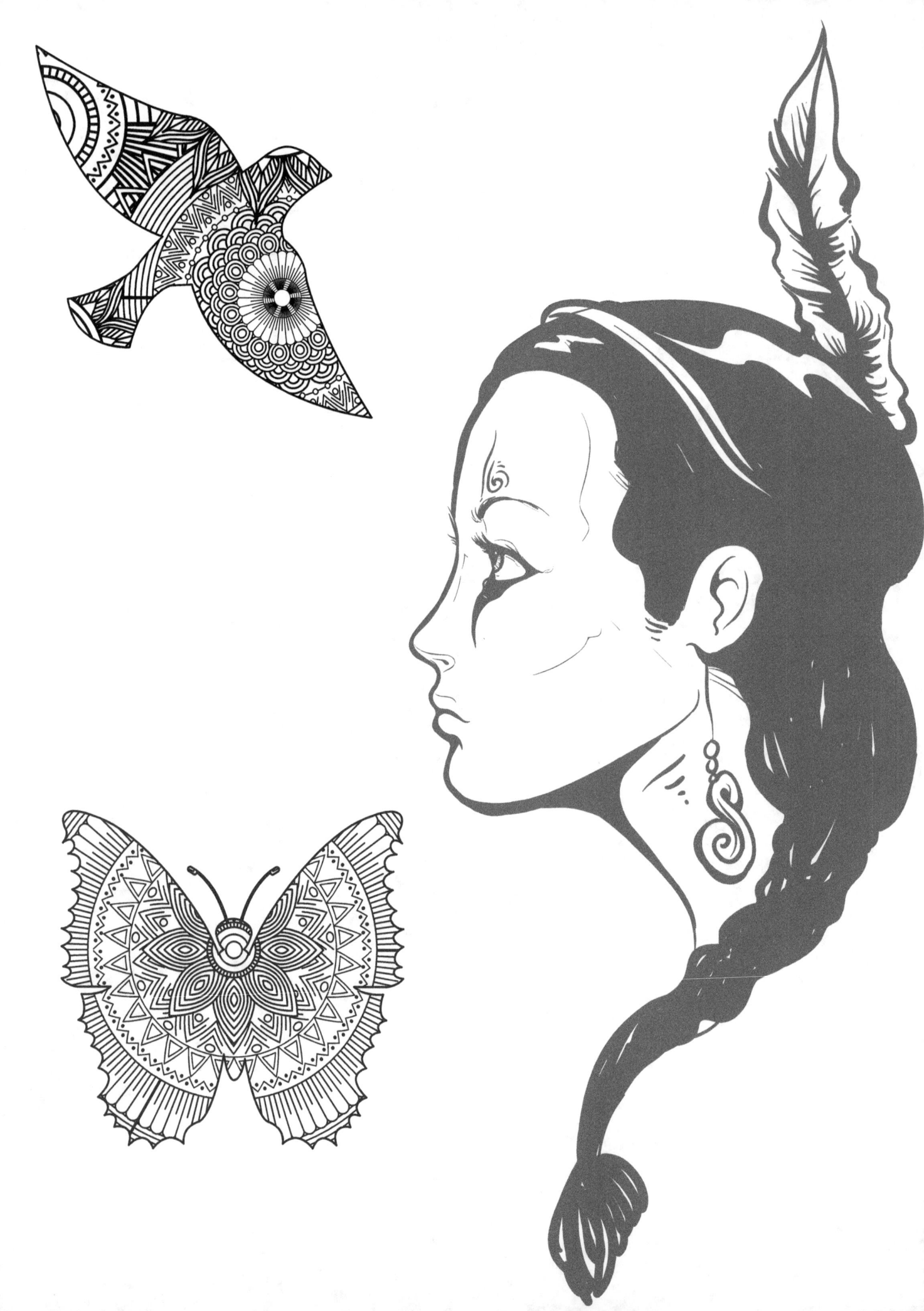

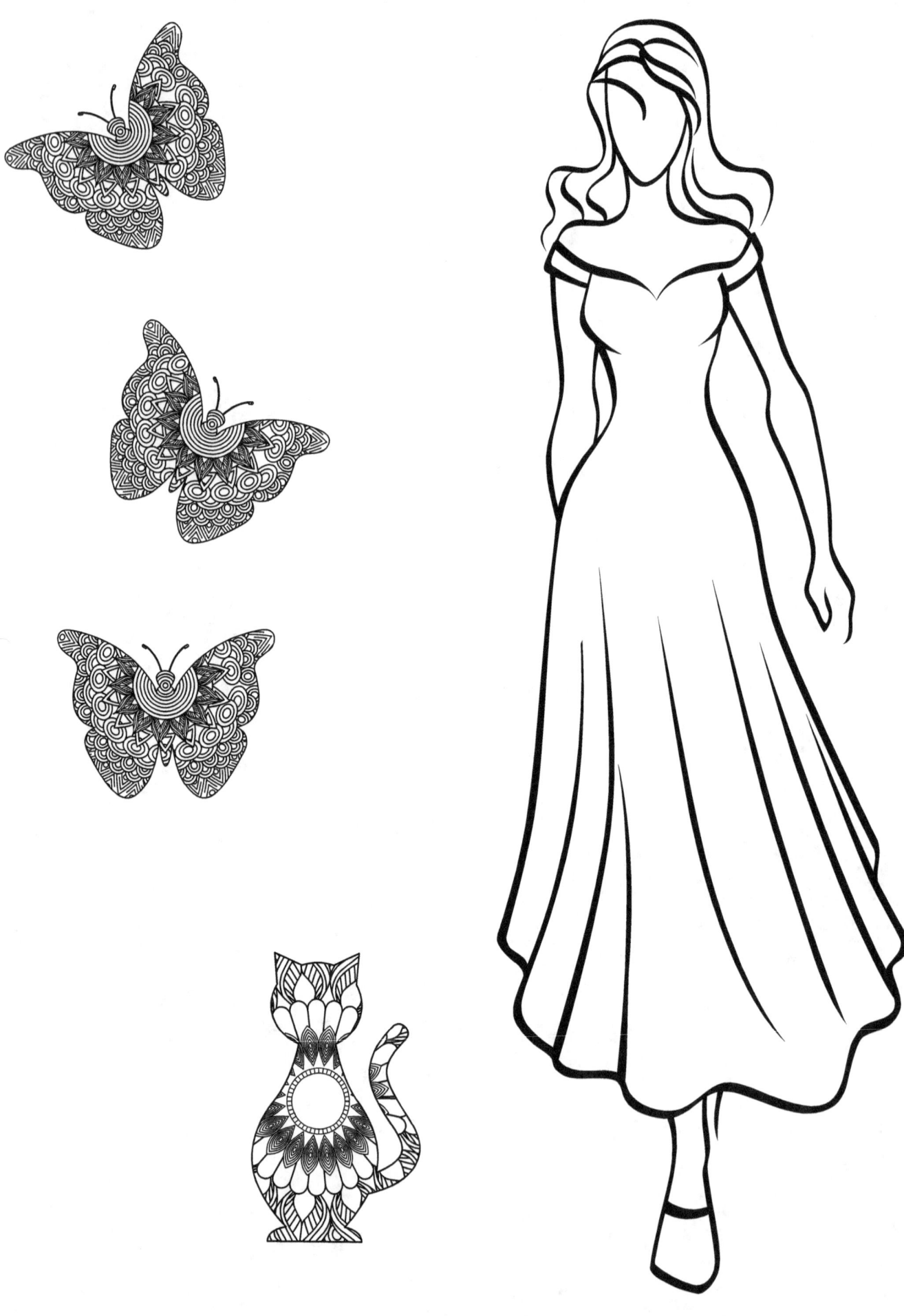

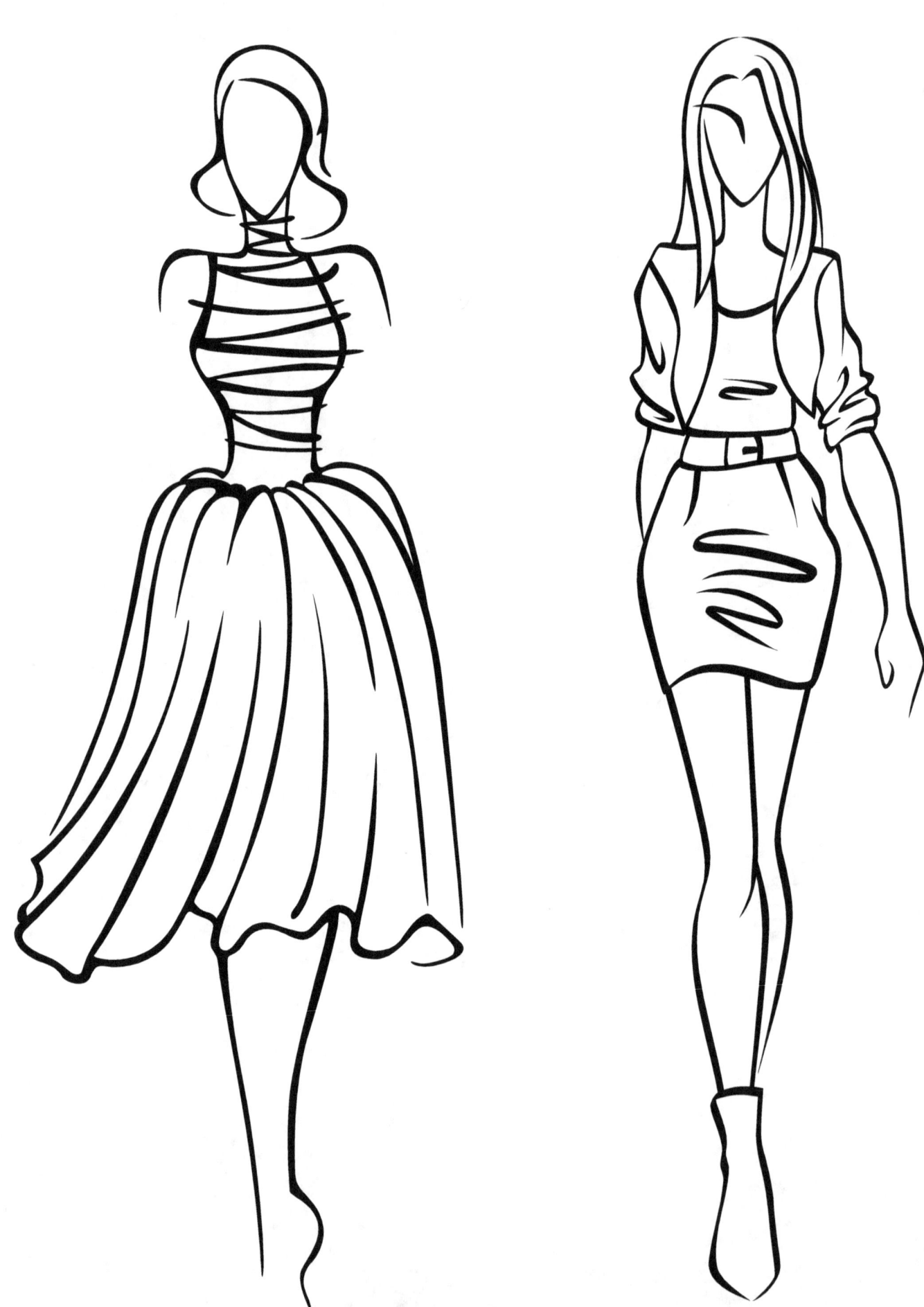

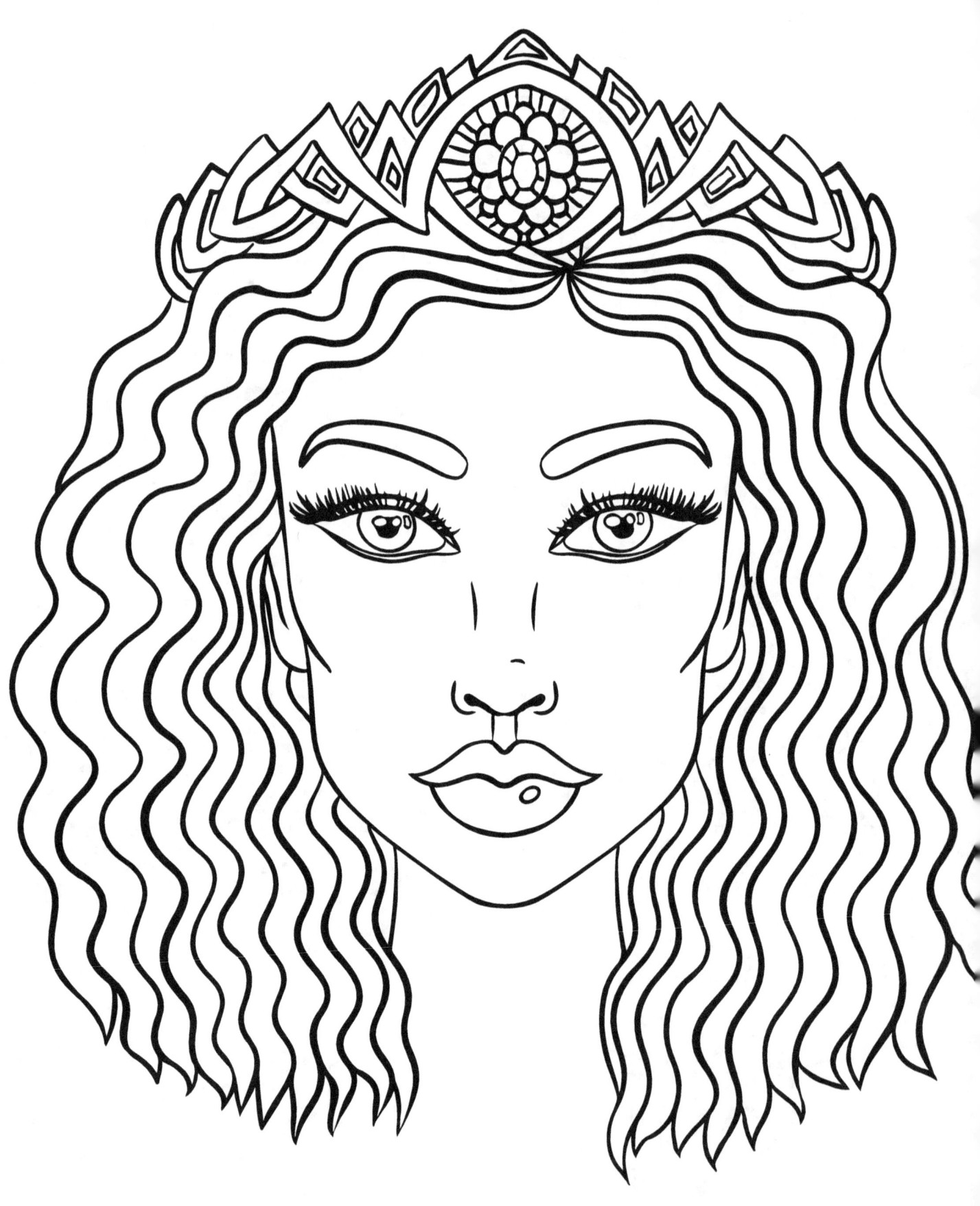

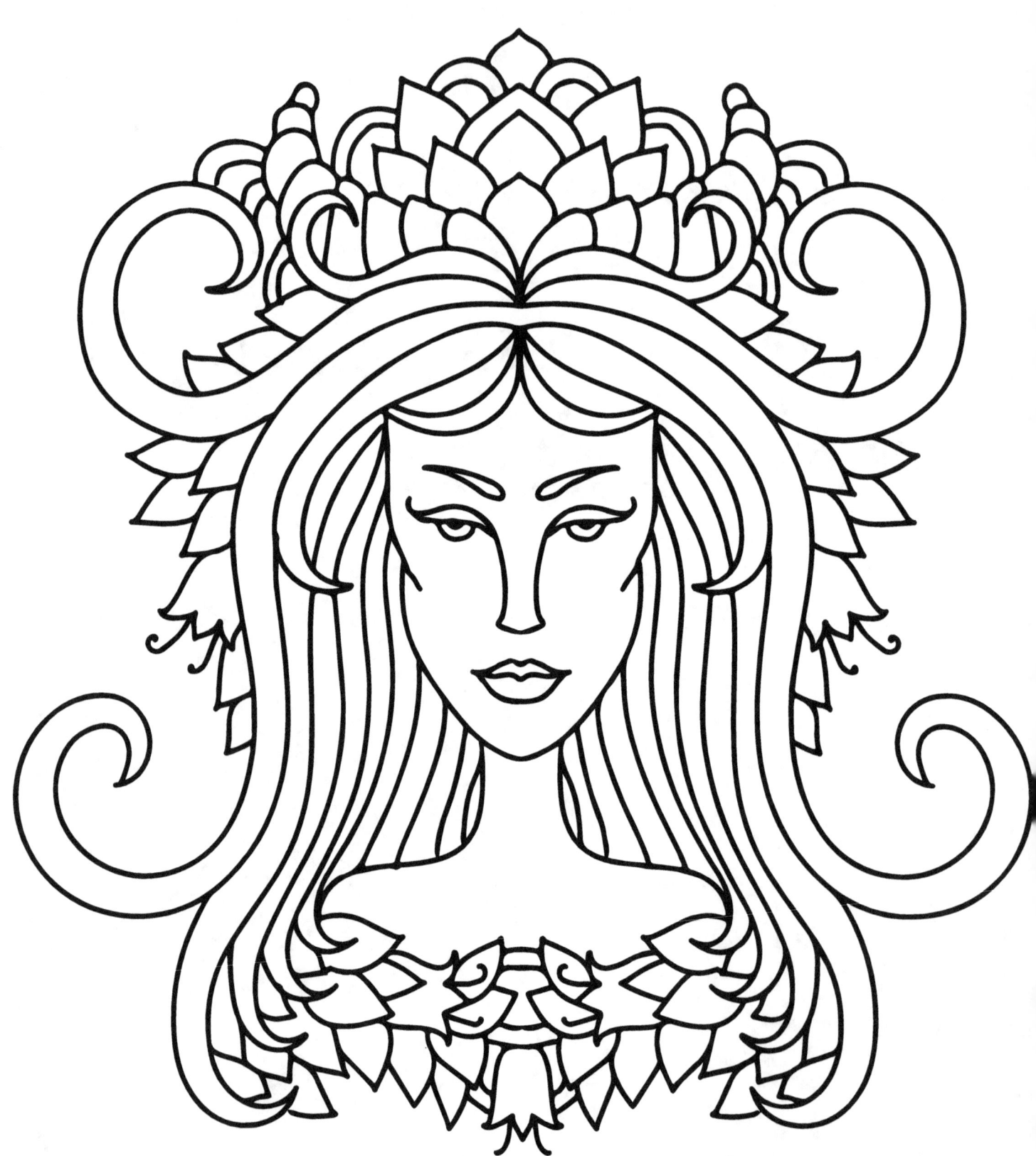

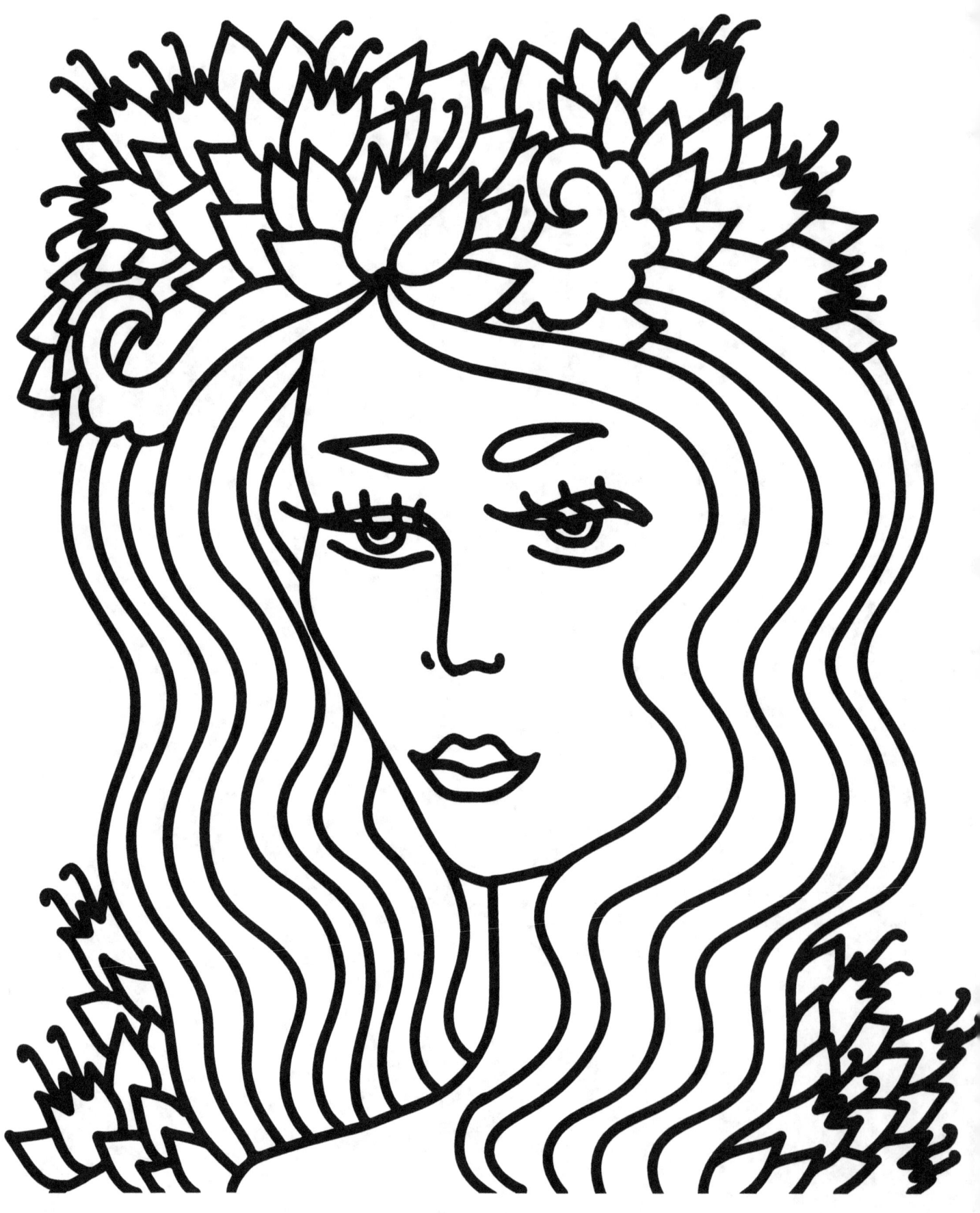

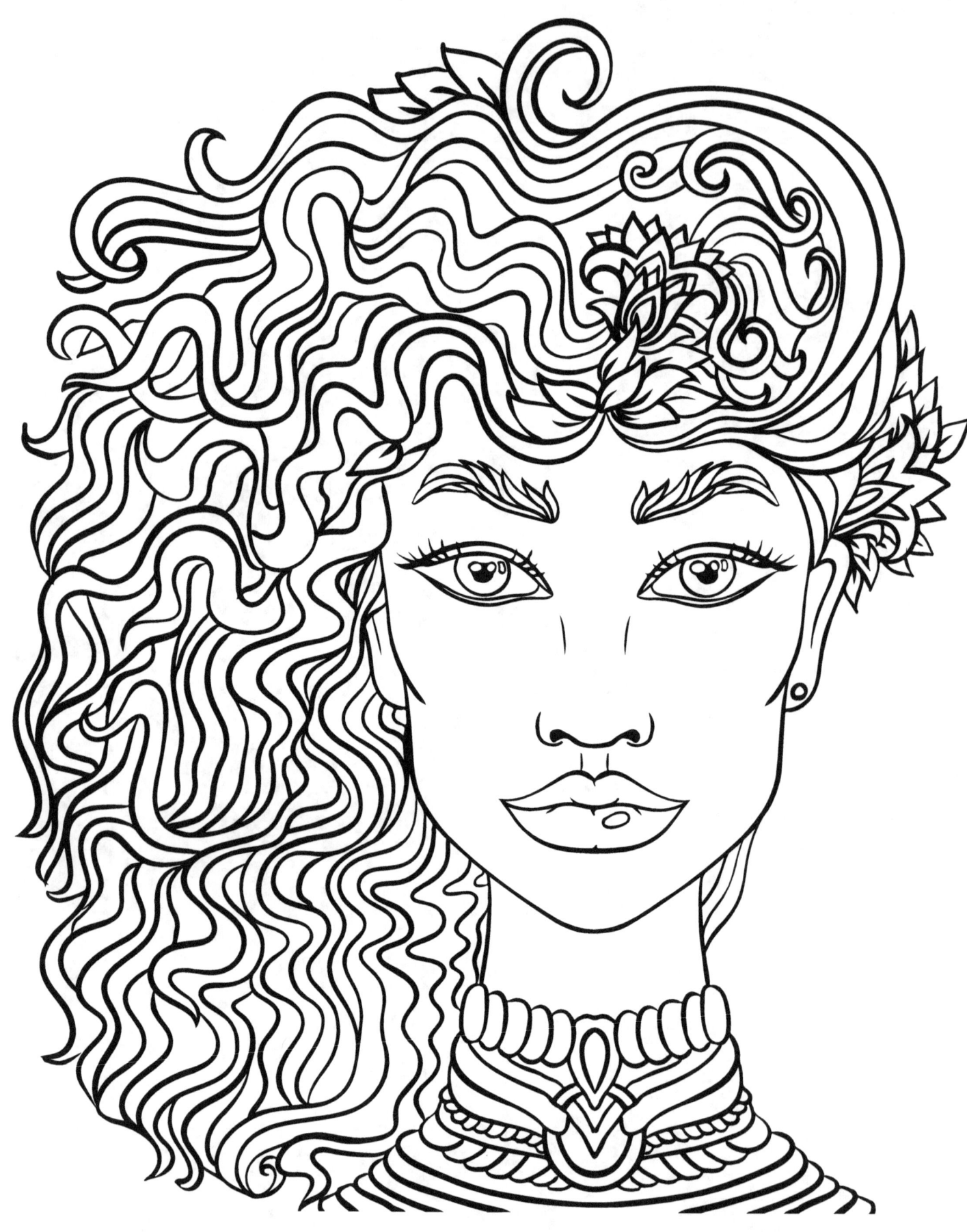

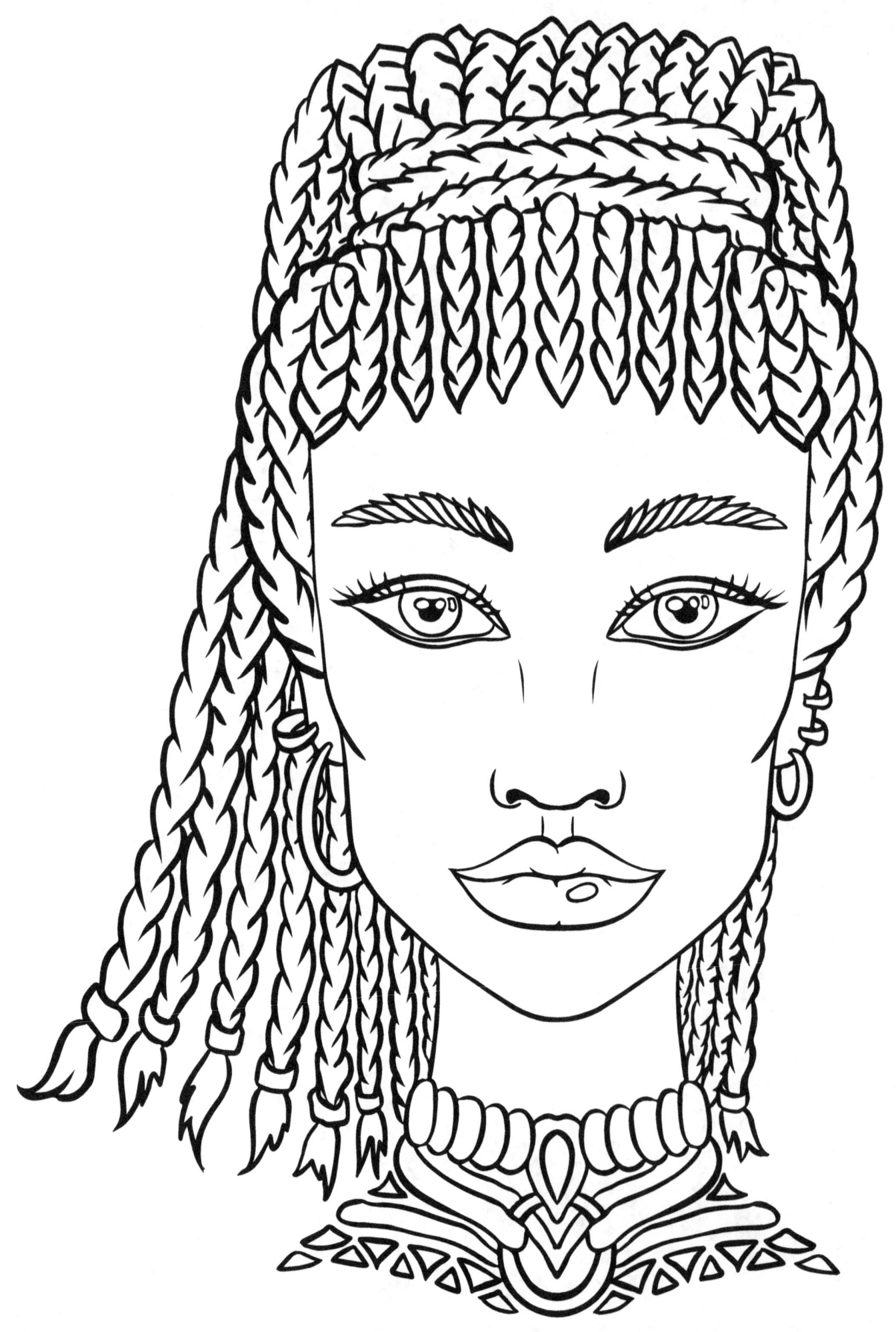

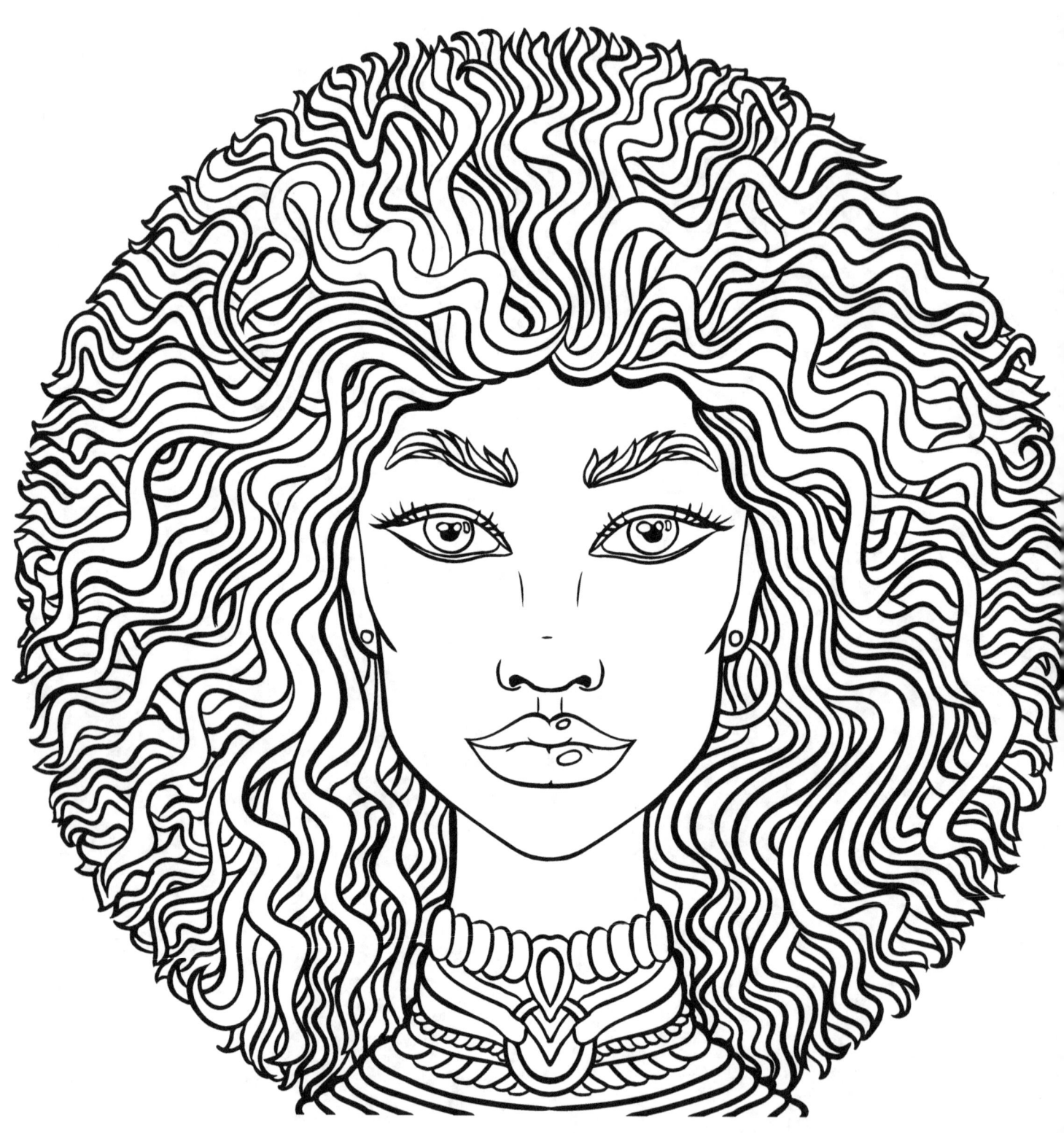

*thank you*

. . . . . . .

www.ingramcontent.com/pod-product-compliance
Lightning Source LLC
Chambersburg PA
CBHW081704220526
45466CB00009B/2876